21

WISDOM

PEARLS

A Guide For
Women In Ministry

Dr. Venice L. McCoy

21 WISDOM PEARLS...A Guide for Women in Ministry

Printed in the United States of America

Library of Congress // United States Copyright Office TXu 1-857-667

Published by:
Eagle-Eye Ministries, Inc.
P.O. Box 734 // Blue Island, IL 60406 // (708) 715-0067
www.eagle-eyeministries.com // eemkc@aol.com
Book design by Venice L. McCoy

ISBN: 978-0-615-86-968-1

Scripture references are from the King James Version.

For additional copies or for use in specialized settings contact:

Dr. Venice L. McCoy
P.O. Box 734 // Blue Island, IL 60406 // (708) 715-0067
www.eagle-eyeministries.com // eemkc@aol.com

Disclaimer: The information contained herein, is not intended to diagnose, treat or cure any medical condition. Always consult a physician before making health decisions.

Contents

Dedication

This book is dedicated to my loving, endearing and most doting mother, *Mother Thelma McCoy*, who successfully carried and birthed the gift of God (me☺). 'Madear', thank you for not miscarrying God's anointed. Thank you for not aborting. Thank you for the gift of life.

This book is also dedicated to the memory of my Spiritual Mom, the late *Dr. Vernice Dandridge-Jones*, who mentored me in ministry. Momma D, I will see you in glory. To the late *Evang. Clara Strong*, the first person to prophesy over my life at age 9 and tell me my destiny.

To the women in Zion who paved the way for women to be whom God purposed and designed women to be.

Introduction

One day my 5 year old niece, Kharis, said to her mom, "mommy the 'mens' preach better." My sister asked her "Kharis, what did you say?" Kharis repeated her statement "the 'mens' preach better mommy." Knowing that Kharis is a HUGE "fan" of my preaching, my sister responded "well, what about TeTe" (as Kharis affectionately calls me)? My darling niece replied "Te Te preach like a man." And to that I laughed hysterically.

Yet, I explored Kharis' statement in greater depth. Many things unfolded from this exploration which led to the inspiration for this book: "21 Wisdom Pearls: A Guide For Women, In Ministry."

My sisters, I've learned many things by error. Some things older women of faith taught me, but many that I share with you penned to the pages of this handbook, were learned by error and by experience.

It is my solemn prayer that the wisdom pearls shared in this handbook will empower you to make full proof of your ministry. I pray that you will diligently fulfill your destiny as a Kingdom daughter. I pray that you will walk in the purpose and plan that God, our Father, has designed and pre-destined for your life. Make a path and help change the world. Make the most of every moment. Don't give your strength to small things. Don't allow tragedies to consume you. You are great, because you are made in the image and likeness of God our Father.

21 Wisdom Pearls

Your Personal Life.

Prayer.

Prayer should be the undisputed number one priority in your life. The only way you can remain faithful during difficult times, when ministry is not going in the direction you think it should, is to keep yourself in a posture or position to hear from the Holy Spirit. That position only comes from a <u>disciplined</u> prayer life. Prayer is the divine connector to move God into your world.

A disciplined prayer life means you develop a lifestyle of prayer. A lifestyle of prayer means you will pray anytime and anywhere and not just a designated time, it means to pray without ceasing {1Thessalonians 5:18}. A <u>lifestyle of prayer</u> takes you beyond praying for God's blessing on a ministry engagement. Yes cover the engagement in prayer (details in wp 3), but this prayer instruction that I share is for YOUR personal development.

Fast.

Set aside a time of monthly fasting or consecration for your <u>personal</u> growth and maintenance. This set time again, is not for a ministry appointment you have (details in wp 3), but for your personal life.

6

Your Personal Life.

Fasting keeps your spirit humble. It keeps you reminded that what you have is a *gift* from God and not something you earned or developed on your own.

Keep a humble spirit and attitude toward the call of God on your life. Having humility equips you with the right spirit to

do the job God has called you to during difficult and challenging times. When there is not ulterior motive of "climbing the ladder" to kingdom success, God will promote you (Psalm 75:6; 1Peter 5:6).

Remember, you are called to the high place of laying down your desires to God's will. Your desire should be to desire the will of God (Jeremiah 29:11). You may have to refresh your spirit of your purpose or motive for doing what you do (Colossians 3:17). It's what I like to call periodic motive checks.

21 Wisdom Pearls

Pearl No. 2
Branding.

We're hearing a lot about Branding today. The word branding simply put, means a marking or calling. Branding is simply the ability to understand your specific gift and to maximize it. It is a 21st century word for what the Apostle Paul shares in 2Timothy 4:5 and what the Apostle Peter shares in 1Peter 1:10.

Paul says to Timothy to do the work of an evangelist and to make full proof of your ministry. He helps Timothy to identify his work, or as we coin it today, his Brand, his calling, his mark. Timothy was a Pastor, with an evangelistic anointing. He was not an evangelist, but his pastoral work focused on evangelism. Timothy's brand is an evangelistic pastor.

Paul goes on to encourage him to make full proof of his ministry, his call, his brand. He's telling him to develop it, be good at it, devote himself to it, and do it well.

Peter's encouragement is similar. He tells us to give diligence to make our calling and election sure. Make your calling or your branding complete. He also

Branding.

encourages us to give diligence to the calling, the branding. Be committed to it and work at it, is what he's telling us. If we work at it, we will never fall, we will be successful.

You, like Timothy, may need some help or direction in understanding or discovering your brand (calling). Be it that your brand is to the healing and deliverance ministry, the prophetic, apostolic, helps, administration, etc., knowing where you are gifted and developing it is very important.

When I first started in ministry, I served in various capacities, which prepared me for each gift of ministry thereafter. For many years I served the kingdom of God as an Evangelist. That gift would prepare my heart with a pure passion for people when I would begin pastoring. Everything that I did prior to now, prepared me for <u>my brand</u>...Pastor with an Apostolic anointing!

So what is your brand? What is your calling? What has God anointed you to do? What are you passionate about that you cannot sleep because you yearn for *it*, because you are hungry for *it*? You will know that *it* is a gift, that *it* is your *brand*, when you are committed to *it* for a lifetime and not just a season. Dear sister, find your gift(s), find your brand, and do *it* well...make full proof.

21 Wisdom Pearls

Pearl No. 3
Accountability.

My sisters, remember it is imperative that you have a spiritual covering. This means you should have son-ship (membership) in a local church assembly. Your membership may not necessarily mean that you attend weekly. If you are a traveling preacher, you are not likely to be in *weekly* attendance. However, that local church is your 'home' church and the leader should have 'an account' of you.

Apostles, Bishops and Pastors, must also be accountable to a leader. People will tell you, just let God be your head. God is your head, but you also need an earthly leader to whom you are accountable.

A leader is necessary:

       1) To watch for your soul {Hebrews 13:17}

       2) To steer your destiny {1Corinthians 4:15}

       3) Pay the tithe and offering

       4) To keep you humble

       5) So that you never forget the art of serving

Accountability.

Many people in ministry have made unnecessary errors because they lacked accountability. Others have had devastating failures because they lacked accountability. They thought having an 'accountability partner' would be sufficient. But the truth is they actually seldom spoke to that person. I believe having a spiritual covering is necessary.

While I am faithful and committed to the church where I serve as Pastor, I am also accountable to the leader I serve. I am always accounted for with my church and leader.

21 Wisdom Pearls

Pearl No. 4
Invitation Protocols.

Wait For An Invitation.

It is not proper decorum and to some pastors even offensive or disgraceful *to invite yourself* to a church, ministry or conference. Sure invite yourself to the prison, hospital, nursing home, streets, but never to a church or ministry. ALWAYS wait for an invitation to minister.

I recall having a fellowship with a Pastor whom I often invited to minister and he would from time to time invite me. But because of pressure from some who wanted to hear me minister at the Pastor's church, I invited myself to preach. The entire tone of his invitation indicated that he did so out of obligation, not because he felt lead of God. I did not feel good about the invite and the ministry results reflected such. It was not one of my most powerful times of ministry there. Years later he shared that he extend invites by the leading of the Holy Spirit.

My sister, WAIT for your invitation. If you don't, you will gain a reputation for being out of order and lose your good name. Lesson learned: WAIT!

Invitation Protocols.

Pray Over Every Invitation.

You should always know the will of God regarding every ministry invitation. <u>People may invite you to come, but God has to release you to go.</u> If you go and it's not the will of God, your time of ministry may not go well. You may even experience unusual demonic activity.

I will never forget a visit to a ministry. It was my first time there. Before introducing me, the Pastor (who was married) stood and said "you all know that this is the first time pastor has ever invited a woman preacher here. She is everything that I ever wanted in a woman." I sat in absolute shock. I could not believe the words I was hearing. It was a horrible experience, because it left the congregation wondering "is there something going on between the two of you?" I got all kinds of strange looks. I did not know this pastor. I had met him through a mutual friend at a funeral. When I received the mic, I preached, let God move and sat down. That was an experience I will *never* forget. That pastor never had good intentions for the invitation, I should have never gone there. <u>Lesson learned</u>: pray over <u>every</u> invitation.

21 Wisdom Pearls

Pearl No. 5
Before Departing.

Pray.

Pray *prior* to travel. Just as personal prayer (wp 1) is important, covering your ministry assignments and appointments with strategic prayer, is vitally important. <u>Strategic prayer will prepare the region and the atmosphere for effective ministry.</u> You want the word of God to be received freely and the time of ministry to be maximized. I have discovered that when strategic prayer has been activated, people will be open to hear the word and there is a smooth flow of the Holy Spirit.

I recall some years ago, while ministering in a city I could not finish the message. I was having a major physical crisis. I barely made it out of the sanctuary and into the restroom. Once in the restroom I was sick to the point that I thought the paramedics may need to be called. I would later conclude this to be an attack of the enemy because after leaving the church, all signs and symptoms of sickness disappeared. This was not the first time I had experienced such an attack.

From that experience, I discovered that whenever I entered that particular time zone, I would come under extreme

Before Departing.

physical attack. I would even experience complications with my flight schedule. Either my flight would be delayed, or I would run late or other issues.

I can't stress enough the importance of praying BEFORE you depart. I learned through terrible experiences the importance to cover EVERY ministry appointment or engagement in prayer.

Sample prayers that I pray: Father God, in the name of Jesus, I decree that as I travel to (city/ministry), souls will be added to your kingdom and revelation will pour forth. Lord God, I decree and thank You in advance, that all demonic activity against me, my health, my sleep, my finances, my mode of transportation and my lodging accommodations, is cancelled in the name of Jesus.

Fast.

Develop a life of consecration, where you set aside a select day(s) every month. This time of consecration may include various types of fasting such as the water only or the Daniel fast. (Note: Always consult a physician).

I especially encourage a fast before going in regions where the area is noted for strongholds and witchcraft. Jesus said in Matthew 17:21 this kind comes out only through prayer and fasting.

21 Wisdom *Pearls*

Pearl No. 6
Never Travel Alone.

Always take someone with you to EVERY ministry engagement. Take an intercessor, an armourbearer, a witness. This may be one person or three separate people. Jesus sent the disciples out in two's, never alone.

Armourbearers.

There are two types of armourbearers: the Old Testament armourbearer, who carries your armour (bags, water, etc.) and the New Testament armourbearer who covers you in the spirit realm, interceding and watching. It is great if one person can be both, but to be highly effective, it is best to have two people to carry out these responsibilities.

My sister, as much as you will try to resist knowing your armourbearer personally, and them knowing you, you must realize that it is unavoidable that you will come to know personal things about one another, especially if your travel together is frequent. Therefore it is crucially important that your armourbearer is a <u>trusted AND mature vessel in the kingdom</u>.

It is important that your armourbearer is mature in the faith:

Never Travel Alone.

1) So they will not share confidential information about you.

2) So that when they see your 'human moments,' and believe me you will have them, they are mature enough to keep quiet, not lose respect, and neither be offended 3) they are able to receive correction.

The armourbearer **must be** well trained and developed. Make sure they are properly prepared to do their job by equipping them with the necessary tools to effectively carry out their responsibilities. They may need books, handbooks, a seminar, conference. Jesus trained His disciples, so be sure to train your armourbearer.

The armourbearer must not have ill motives for serving. For example, some will want to be seen with the preacher, want to get their name out there, or even want "personal time." They cannot be a Gehazi (2Kings 5) who wants the goods and is willing to lie on the leader, to get them. The armourbearer must be willing to serve with a servant's heart.

One final word on the armourbearer, be kind to those who assist you. Do not mistreat them or take them for granted. I've had some really good help and through a lack of wisdom, drove them away. Good, anointed, faithful, armourbearers and assistants are hard to come by in today's church.

21 Wisdom *Pearls*

Pearl No. 7
Office Protocols.

Wait For The Pastor.

NEVER enter a Pastor's office without his or her invitation. I'll never forget being in a city and arriving before the pastor. The usher escorted me to the pastor's office. When the pastor arrived he said to me "what are you doing in my office? Never enter a pastor's office without <u>their</u> invitation." That pastor was a dear friend of mine and he laughed after saying it, though I could tell he was very serious. I thanked him for the "tip." I have never forgotten those words or that experience.

I'll never forget the young lady who entered my office without my permission. She accidentally knocked over some books, breaking my lamp. She apologized and offered to replace the lamp. I said it was ok. She insisted and after I explained it was a gift, she felt worse and said "I have learned a lesson to never go in a pastor's office."

I should add that if the pastor has given you permission in advance to use his or her office in their absence, then go for it, otherwise, wait.

Office Protocols.

Never Enter Alone.

Having your armourbearer with you in the office ensures accountability (details wp 3). I recall ministering at a church and being invited to the Pastor's office. My armourbearer was seated in the sanctuary. As I entered the office, the pastor was dressing and proceeded to do so in front of me. Though it was only his outer shirt, this was inappropriate. I kindly placed myself outside of the door until he was ready to enter the sanctuary. This was a lesson well learned. Never enter alone.

21 Wisdom Pearls

Pearl No. 8
K.I.S.S.

Be sure to properly define relationships in ministry. Some and most I even say, you should K.I.S.S. (keep it strictly spiritual). It is simply impossible to be "friends" with every Pastor you meet.

Also **avoid** establishing friendships with individuals you meet at a ministry. (A lesson learned the hard way). If an individual is assigned to you as an armourbearer or to transport you while visiting a ministry, be sure that alone is your relationship with them.

I recall ministering in a city and becoming good friends with the person assigned to me. Well, as my Kingdom assignment became greater and I developed more responsibilities, my time became very restrictive. I had to redefine and reprioritize all of my relationships. The sister with whom I had become *good friends*, I redefined as a *casual friend*, because she would consume a lot of my time.

My decision did not settle in agreement with her and she would later become very hostile towards me, because she could no longer access me as she once had. It resulted in not only the ending of the friendship, but also the closing

K.I.S.S.

of the door to that ministry. The dear sister slandered my name and made false accusations about me to her pastor. I tried reconciling the fellowship, but whether it was pride or something else, the pastor never responded. The truth of her character later surfaced and the pastor had to remove her from areas of the ministry. I settled in my spirit that all was well and that I had learned a valuable lesson to keep it strictly spiritual (k.i.s.s.).

I have also come to understand why many ministers do not greet the congregation after they have ministered. People will ask for your card wanting to know if they can call you later because 'I just need someone to talk to,' or 'I need some direction.' Their claims maybe valid but God did not send you there for *one-on-one* ministry. You shared all that God intended for you to tell them during your 30 minutes across the mic. Many times laity will not understand this or they are in defiance. I recall being at a ministry and someone approaching me after the service asking for a personal prophecy. I shared this with the pastor and he said to me "Dr. McCoy, I cannot tell you how many times I have told our people not to bother the preacher when the have finished ministering." I now make it my habit to go directly to the office and not greet the people to avoid such encounters.

One last note, remember that the anointing is attractive. Some brothers and yes sisters also, will try to cross the spiritual line, so you must K.I.S.S.

21 Wisdom Pearls

Pearl No. 9
<u>Keep It Simple.</u>

Sisters there's nothing more egregious than a complicated ministry guest with requests that become intrusive. While I believe you should be treated well by your host, you are not the center of purpose...CHRIST is. You are anointed because of the anointed one...CHRIST. When you are invited to minister keep your requests simple. After all, no one is *obligated* to invite you to come and share. There are many anointed vessels that God can send.

I share this because there are some ministers of the gospel who have gained a reputation for being complicated, difficult, and having a long list of requirements in order to come minister. This reputation has cost them some invitations. As a pastor, I know I have declined to invite some to minister once I saw their long and <u>unnecessary</u> list of requirements. Remember that you are going to ***minister***, <u>not on vacation</u>. Please allow me to share the following recommendations.

Beverage

Refrain from being complex in your request. If you drink freshly squeezed juice, the ministry will not likely have a

Keep It Simple.

juice extractor on site. If 'fresh juice' is a desire/or dietary requirement, you may need to bring your own juice. I've carried my own juice for years and still do. Why have I placed emphasis here? You would be surprised how difficult and yes, even how ugly, preachers can be about this.

Hospitality Suites (Post-Service Fellowship).

The same rule applies as with the beverage. Refrain from being complex with your requests. If you have dietary restrictions, simply and <u>kindly</u> decline the meal or kindly place a simple request. Do not offend your hosts.

I recall being in a city once and was new to my lifestyle of having dietary restrictions. After service, there had been an elaborate meal prepared at the Pastor's home. The meal consisted mostly of fried foods. In compliance with my diet, I only ate the vegetables. Soon I was asked why I was eating nothing else. Rather than giving a simple "I have dietary restrictions," I went into a LONG explanation that I don't think was shared in the *kindest* tone. In hindsight, I think I probably offended my host.

While I didn't make any special requests or have a long list, the results of my explanation were the same...obtrusive. Sure I had valid health reasons, but **how** I responded was the issue. I will never forget *that* experience. Lesson of simplicity surely learned.

21 Wisdom Pearls

Pearl No. 10
Ministerial Graces.

Many in ministry should learn and understand the importance of ministerial graces.

Be kind.

This is a fruit of the spirit. (Galatians 5:22 – moral *excellence* in character or demeanor).

Be polite, gentle and meek.

2Timothy 2:24 lets us know that as servants of the Lord we are to be gentle to everyone. Some ministries you travel to will not have arrived to the level of excellence that you NOW have knowledge of. They may not know how to entreat men and women of God with hospitality (Romans 12:13, 1 Peter 4:9).

I cannot tell you how many times my accommodations, from hotel, to transportation, to reservations, etc., were not in the spirit of excellence. I remained polite, gentle, patient and meek, understanding that they had not 'arrived.'

Ministerial Graces.

Be firm.

Being kind and polite does not mean you are not to be firm and strong.

Reply to invitations in a timely manner.

Ensure that your ministry invitation process explains the length of time for reply. Whether your invitations are frequent or few, using a ministry request form may be necessary. Also, when you are inviting guests to minister, give yourself proper planning time (8-12 weeks).

Say "thank you."

The word of God instructs us as believers to be kind to each other (Ephesians 4:32). I regularly send a thank you letter to the ministry that invited me. Also, when someone recommends you, be sure to thank them.

21 Wisdom Pearls

Pearl No. 11
Never Male Bash.

I simply do not believe that God has called us to fight against one another in the body of Christ (Galatians 5:15). While there is sexism in the church, we must remember that the Apostle Paul informed us in Galatians 3:28, there is no gender when it comes to the kingdom of God, because we are one in Christ Jesus.

A wise woman once told me to never 'defend' the call of God on my life. She went on to tell me "you are not invited to stand there and explain away that God has called women to preach." I've applied that counsel for years, and watched it work for me. Many times women try to 'defend' or 'explain' that God has called women into the Kingdom. This is unhealthy because that attempt leads to 'one man up man ship,' putting our brothers down to lift ourselves up or the explanation ends in a dissertation of degrading the brothers in the faith.

When the pastor who had wrong motives for inviting me (details wp 3), introduced me, I stood to preach never acknowledging or even addressing his statement. My lack of addressing it, was to ensure I gave his actions no power,

Never Male Bash.

but also to ensure that I did not belittle him as a leader in his house. I stood and preached and let the power of God be on display.

Dr. McCoy, are you saying to ignore the divide? In short, I am saying do not give your strength to this issue, nor use the sacred desk to address it. Your addressing the divide across the sacred desk will result in:

1) You gain a reputation as a woman who bashes men in the kingdom.

2) Gaining a reputation as hating men.

3) Gaining a reputation as being bitter and scorned.

4) No one wanting to hear you preach. People do not go to services to hear a 'fussing' or angry preacher. They are there to be encouraged and edified.

5) Closing of ministry doors for yourself.

One final note, resist the temptation to get into groups with women whose entire purpose of meeting is to discuss the unfair treatment of the brothers towards the sisters. As long as there is winter and summer, cold and heat, this issue will stand. You simply fulfill what God has called you to do and leave the rest to God.

21 Wisdom Pearls

Pearl No. 12
Encourage the Leadership.

My spiritual mom told me to always be sure to promote the Pastor. What she simply meant was build and strengthen that leader when you are at a ministry. Encourage the saints to thank God for their godly leader. Encourage the household of faith to be faithful and appreciate the gift of God given to their local house.

Encourage the people of God to walk in obedience to the one who has the rule over them. (Hebrews 13:7, 17). Speak faith-filled positive words that build the house and leadership.

Encourage the saints to undergird and support their leader by supporting the vision and running with the vision God has assigned to the house (Habakkuk 2:2). Ensure them that when they keep in pace with the leader, anointing will be made available for them to effectively carry out the vision with godly strength and surety.

Remind the saints of the blessing of serving in the kingdom of God. It seems the art of serving is a forgotten

Encourage The Leadership.

ministry gift in today's church (Romans 12:7). Encourage them to keep a godly attitude in their service and to remain humble, and God will promote them in due season.

Encourage the saints of that local assembly to work together, supporting each area of ministry so that the entire house may be effectual.

Finally remind them that they are there in that ministry because God planted them there, and to bloom where they have been planted. If you do these things, it will surely bring strength and encouragement to the Pastor.

21 Wisdom Pearls

Pearl No. 13
Your Business.

Taking care of business is important and brings promotion (Proverbs 22:9).

Arrive on time.

Even if the ministry is notorious for starting late, you arrive on time because God sees you and holds you accountable to time (Romans 12:11).

Bio.

Develop your ministerial bio, resume, business cards and ministry request form. Carry your cards with you, but wait to be asked for it. If you are not a pastor, you may want to include your church affiliation on the card so that it shows you have accountability.

Expenses.

Count up the cost for out of town travels (Luke 14:28). Gain a clear understanding from the inviting ministry as to what expenses they will cover <u>BEFORE</u> you leave your city. If necessary, ask <u>what</u> they will pay for. Here's a starter list:

Your Business.

- Airfare?

- Hotel?

- Your assistant's airfare/hotel?

- Ground transportation. Who will pick you up from the airport? (I have been left at airports and told to get the shuttle or a taxi…lesson learned the hard way.)

- Is the person picking you up physically able to load, unload, carry your luggage?

- How will you (and your assistant) be transported to the service? (This many not be the same person who provided transportation from the airport).

- If necessary, how will you get around the city? Will a driver be available?

- Is there reimbursement for meals or is a meal stipend provided?

- If the event is a banquet, will your assistant's meal be complimentary or will they be expected to pay? (I have been told my assistant needed to pay. It should be complimentary.)

21 Wisdom Pearls

Pearl No. 14
Your Honorarium.

No Arguments.

Never squabble about an offering. My motto is that God will make up the difference to you. I have not always been treated fairly, but I promise you God has ALWAYS made it up to me, because ultimately, I work for God.

I have not always had this perspective. I recall once asking if a ministry could assist a little more because of the travel expenses I'd incurred getting to their event. The pastor became very livid and near hostile with me. I didn't know about wisdom pearl no. 13 at the time. I had paid my own expenses assuming I would be reimbursed. As it would turn out, the honorarium would not even be equivalent to my travel expenses. I gently backed away from the request knowing that I was not going to receive any more than I already had. That was a lesson well learned.

Check for Integrity.

Check your envelope to be sure it is filled before you leave. My spiritual mom told me "baby, check your envelope." I wasn't sure why she was telling me to do so,

Your Honorarium.

but I did. She said "I have made it home and my envelope was empty." I was aghast that people in the kingdom would operate with such low or no integrity.

Amount.

When asked if you have an honorarium, give an answer. If it is yes, *kindly* share it.

If it no, here's a few responses you can give. You can reply "no, but I do have an amount I am accustomed to," or "I do not have an honorarium, but I do have an expectation."

Advise the ministry to whom the check should be made payable to. There may be times when the Holy Spirit may instruct you not to receive an honorarium.

21 Wisdom Pearls

Your Dress.

1. Dress appropriately for ministering.

2. If you do not know the dress code of the ministry or the event, simply ask, or you may include it as a question on your ministry information form.

3. Dress appropriately for the occasion. You do not want to overdress nor under dress.

4. NEVER, let me again say <u>never</u> wear a clergy collar with a sequined or rhinestone suit. It is inappropriate, not to mention gaudy.

5. Do not wear tight, revealing, see-through, low cut or cleavage showing clothing. This removes the attention from your message and places it on you the messenger. Remember you are there to minister, not for a fashion show nor to be sexy. Turn in your 'diva card' when you hit the sacred desk.

6. Even if the attire is casual, leggings are never appropriate for a minister to wear on stage.

Your Dress.

7. 'Tighten' it up where necessary. Make sure nothing is "jiggling." Embrace wearing body firming garments.

8. Although many women have left off of wearing nylons today, I think in many settings they are still appropriate.

9. If you perspire when ministering, take a change of clothing. You should change regardless of weather conditions.

   ▪ Change into *appropriate* clothing.

   ▪ If you are not offered an office, change in the restroom. I certainly have!

10. Don't forget your hat and scarf in the winter.

21 Wisdom Pearls

Pearl No. 16
Your Hygiene and Health.

Breath.

Do a breath check. Make sure it is fresh at ALL times.

Personal ministry. Make sure your breath is fresh when you are ministering to people up close and personal. There is nothing worse than receiving a prophecy from a preacher who has major halitosis issues.

After message mint. Do breath checks after you minister, before greeting people or entering the hospitality suite, you may need a mint. I do recommend breath mints that are all natural. Artificial ingredients will lower your immune system's ability to work and not good for your overall health. These can be purchased at most health food stores.

Body.

Bathing/Showering. It is extremely important to have good body decorum, as a lifestyle, but especially for professionals who have contact with the public. Preacher, you should be CLEAN and FRESH. Your hygiene has an impact on your mood, motivation and inspiration.

Your Hygiene and Health.

If you perspire heavily, change your garments after ministering, before greeting. Always clean your garments after preaching, particularly if you perspire. It is **not** good hygiene to wear it again if it has not been <u>cleaned</u>.

Fragrance.

If you wear perfume, it should be in moderation and not overpowering. If you smell your perfume, 5 hours after application as strongly as when you applied it, it is likely that you applied too much and it may be offensive to your public.

Be careful not to apply too much fragranced hand creams. If you are one who lays hands in prayer, you are likely to transfer that fragrance. Again, this may be offensive to your public.

Incontinence.

If you have an incontinence problem, be sure to secure this area before you minister. Some sisters have reported 'tiny tinkles' right in the middle of the message. Wear a device <u>designed specifically</u> for incontinence.

Your Hygiene and Health.

Beverage.

Avoiding beverages with artificial sugars has become a practice of mine. All natural gives more energy.
I have discovered that artificial sugar shuts down the immune system, making your body susceptible to germs and viruses. For hot tea, you may want to use raw honey.

Energy.
I've discovered that squeezing ½ an orange into a glass of water energizes me and restore electrolytes I lose while preaching. I use the orange instead of an energy drink. I also take B-complex to help relieve stress on my body since I travel often and preach hard. You should always consult a physician before making any health changes.

21 Wisdom Pearls

Pearl No. 17
Your Rest.

Getting the proper rest is essential to the body. Ministering is not only spiritual work, but physical work as well. Ministering requires the participation of our bodies. I've said it for years…we need these bodies to transport the anointing.

Resting your body on the day of ministry is essential to being able to maximize your time of ministry. You may need to reprioritize your check list for that particular day. You do not want to arrive at your ministry appointment exhausted and not have high impact. How you feel impacts how you minister.

So often, I travel to different cities, and I'm offered touring opportunities, but I know I must decline. I will even decline going to lunch (which can turn into a 3 hour outing). I gently decline and kindly explain that I want to be fully prepared to minister for the service that night.

I'll never forget my very first time traveling out of town to minister. I had a friend in the neighboring state. I spent the day traveling two hours each way, once there touring and walking. When I returned to my hotel I was beat.

Your Rest.

When I rose to preach that night, I was exhausted and had very little physical strength to preach. I should have had my friend to come meet me. A lesson well learned.

I cannot stress enough the importance of getting the proper rest. Establish a personal Sabbath (time of rest and personal worship), be it full or half day. This is a commandment that the church is responsible to keep, but many today, do not. I am convinced a personal Sabbath will extend your life.

21 Wisdom Pearls

Pearl No. 18
Your Temple.

My sisters take care of your body which is the temple of the Holy Ghost. I shared in the previous wisdom pearl, that we need these bodies to transport the anointing. Your diet is a huge factor in taking care of your body. A healthy diet will produce longevity in life and in ministry. Over the years, I've had to change my diet in order to have maximum energy when I minister.

The following are suggestions for a healthy temple and not intended to diagnose or treat any health problems. Always consult your physician for dietary changes.

I practice a dietary lifestyle that includes live foods, i.e. fresh fruit, vegetables, freshly squeezed juices. My meat is baked cold-water fish. For me, this lifestyle is producing my desired results of good health and energy. I have intentionally excluded what I consider dead foods from my diet, i.e. artificial products, packaged foods, etc. See wisdom pearl no. 9 for maintaining your health as you travel.

A healthy diet is evident in your appearance, your skin,

Your Temple.

your hair, your nails, etc. If you take vitamin supplements, remember they are just that and not a substitution for healthy eating.

Be sure to incorporate some exercise in your daily life. Keep those limbs agile and strong.

My precious sisters, so many of you will really appreciate this next bit of wisdom. Many have wondered "when it's that time of the month, do I still minister?" I say use discretion and wisdom (Proverbs 2:11). If you MUST go, be sure your "first garments" (pads) are properly secured. <u>Also, determine how hard **and** long you will be able to preach.</u>

Women who have irregularities due to fibroids or endometriosis or other issues, will have to be extremely careful about ministering during your flow. I have experienced such an issue and it does interfere with your time of ministry. That is why I am able to tell you first-hand that we need these bodies to transport the anointing. My sister, please take care of your temple.

21 Wisdom Pearls

Pearl No. 19
Your Voice.

1. I try to eliminate 'stress' on my voice when ministering, by always warming it up first. I use warm water with a slice of fresh lemon. This works well <u>for me</u>.

2. I avoid drinking cold beverages before, while and right after I minister. I have discovered that cold beverages constricts my vocal cords. When drinking while ministering, I always make sure my beverage is room temperature.

3. On extremely rare occasions I may become hoarse. If so, I mix together green tea, ¼ capsule of cayenne pepper and raw honey. This works well <u>for me</u>.

4. When traveling in a car with the person who is transporting you from the airport or to a service, do not be afraid to kindly ask them to adjust the heat/air. Air and heat levels may impact your voice and thus your ability to minister.

5. If you are a 'hooper' never start your key too high because you will have nowhere to modulate

Your Voice.

(climb). Also note, that staying in a high key too long may place stress on your vocal cords and result in you becoming hoarse.   Always preach from your diaphragm and not your throat. This will allow you to smoothly and successfully ascend the key scale. It will also keep you from:

      1) straining

      2) sounding like you're screaming

      3) damaging your vocal chords

      4) becoming hoarse.

21 Wisdom Pearls

Pearl No. 20
Your Message.

Preparation.

Pray: seek God for the message for HIS people. Prophets and Traveling Preaching may carry the same message for a season.

Meditation/Consecration Time: over the Word that God has given you.

Fast: as an ongoing minister, develop a common fast time.

Study: Commit proper time. Even if you know the subject well, revisit it to see if God will give you fresh revelation.

Worship: Very important and key to keeping the flesh humbled.

Composing the Message.

Preach the Word only: (John 3:34 & 7:18, 1Peter 4:11, John 6:63, 68, Mark 8:38, Matthew 24:35)

Your Message.

Resources: Do not be afraid to use resources other than the Bible (i.e. Bible dictionary/encyclopedia, experts on the subject, books, etc., but ultimately only include what God wants in the message). Make sure information you find is truth.

Tailor the Message accordingly: Revival, Crusade, Conference, Convention, Seminar, Workshop, Symposium, Multi-speaker, Special Occasion, Anniversary, Women's Day, etc. Are you one of multiple speakers, the keynote or only speaker? This determines your allotted time. Is it a morning, afternoon or evening service? This also determines your allotted time.

Subject.

Confidence: KNOW your subject.

Conviction: Feel your subject. Feel what God is speaking. God speaks to your spirit, mind and ear.

Consistency: Stick with your subject whether teaching or preaching. Don't give the audience what I call a jambalaya message, mixing 3 messages in one. The people will leave with no idea as to what you preached.

Your Message.

Connection: Keep your audience reminded of the subject by making reference to it during the message.

Compliance: Preach the given theme. If the occasion has a theme, your message should be centered around that theme.

Text.

Context: Be contextual (do not use a Scripture out of context). Use supporting Scriptures contextually (1Thessalonians 5:21).

Key verse(s). Highlight or state key verse(s). The only time that I use more than 3-5 verses from a passage is in Revival, Seminar, or Workshop. You may make reference to more, but reading them will cut into your allotted time.

Personal Interest.

Make the message applicable to your audience. Apply the word of God to today's believers and their lives.

Use examples, i.e. scriptural references, personal testimonies, your or other's.

Drive It Home.

Make sure the message is cohesive.   Tie it altogether, making sure there is a flow. Avoid taking too long to

Your Message.

reach the heart of your message. You will lose your audience even if your message is good. Further, 21st century saints are not going to sit through a 2 hour preacher. Much further, you will wear your body into sickness. Preaching 1 hour and working the altar 1 hour, is hard work and wears on the body. For the preacher who ministers often, two hours of ministering, is not sound wisdom.

Presentation Method.

Preacher, Teacher, both. Know whether you are a preacher, teacher or a combination of both perhaps with one having greater strength.

Be balanced in your message.

Model but do not duplicate your leader/mentor.

Avoid using "tell your neighbor" repeatedly. After all, we didn't come to service to talk to our neighbor.

Above all, BE ANOINTED.

Keep It Positive.

Do not 'beat' the people up when you're preaching. Correction is the Pastor's job, unless you are flowing under a Prophetic or Apostolic mantle to foster winds of

Your Message.

change and reconciliation. Even then, there is a way to bring correction without being abusive, wounding and even condescending. The Apostle Paul says in 2Corinthians 10:8, that his authority was given to edify the saints and not for their destruction. He adds in 2Corinthians 13:10, even if he should use sharpness, it is to edification, not destruction.

No one wants to leave a worship service feeling as though they have just been attacked. No one leaves the comforts of home or a long work day to arrive to hear a 'fussing' preacher. My sister, remember that your ministry assignment in any house has an end goal to edify, exhort and comfort (1Corinthians 14:13).

One last note, the sacred desk is not to be used as a vantage point to "get anyone straight." It is not to be used to degrade other ministers of the gospel. My dear sisters, please, never desecrate the sacred desk with such behavior. PREACH THE GOSPEL, minister and sit down!

21 Wisdom Pearls

Pearl No. 21
Don't Quit.

With more than 1,700 ministers quitting the ministry each month, I encourage you my precious and dear sister in the faith, to stand strong and firm in your calling. [Isaiah 50:7]. Do not be intimidated by the wicked one. Woman of God, you have always been Satan's enemy [Genesis 3:15].

Throughout the Bible, the leaders that moved the strongest with God, understood the times in which they lived [1Chronicles 12:32]. Understand the assignment of God on your life for every season and move forward.

Take no prisoners! Don't worry about who's not with you or who leaves. Some people are sent for a season. Neither should you worry over who doesn't like you, or how many haters you have. You need haters, otherwise God can't set a table before you in their presence (Psalm 23:5). Further, Jesus said you would be hated (Matthew 10:22).

Quitting must never be an option. Square your shoulders and fight like Deborah [Judges 4]…victoriously. You are a now generation leader. You have been called into the Kingdom of God for such a time as this and no devil in hell can stop in you! Rise up and answer the call!

My Prayer For You.

Gracious Father full of all wisdom, it is in the name of Jesus, the Christ that I pray. I lift up the Kingdom preacher whose hands hold this book. Father, I speak Your love, peace, joy, strength and wisdom upon her now. I ask that she experience You in a brand new and fresh way in her ministry as a result of reading this book. I ask that You make my sister an example for other preachers in the kingdom to model.

I cancel spirits that have held her hostage from advancing to your original design for her life. I loose perfected destiny upon her now. I ask for continual guidance by the Holy Spirit in everything she does.

I cancel physical attacks, spiritual attacks, mental and emotional attacks. I cancel generational curses. I pray that her prayer life, fast life, and study life be multiplied. I pray for the advancing of their finances as You teach her to be a good steward over all that You bring into her possession. Strengthen Lord God, her peace, patience and persistence.

Preacher, I release the angels of God to protect you, shield you and cover you in your going out and in your coming in. May goodness, mercy, wisdom and favor be your caretakers.

My Prayer For You.

My dear sister, may the God of peace, love, wisdom and revelation, cause you to multiply and abound in His inheritance for your life.

I pray that He will take you through your transitions to bring reformation to every area of your life. May the God of the former and the latter rain be multiplied unto you.

I speak to you, Preacher of the Most High God, that the lion within you releases the boldness to possess the land. No longer shall you be timid and intimidated. No longer shall you walk in fear. I break the spirit of restriction and limitation that caused you to lose focus. I declare that now is your breakthrough. I speak to you now woman of God, to arise with the anointing of the sons of Issachar to fulfill your God-given assignment.

As you have read this book and now read this prayer, I decree and declare that a new day has dawned upon you and your ministry. I declare the old systems and old methodologies and mentality, be broken off of you. I declare fresh oil, new wineskin and a new wine upon you.

In Jesus' name. Amen.

Life Improvement Pearls.

Wisdom Pearl No. _____

Plan of action:

_____

_____

_____

_____

Wisdom Pearl No. _____

Plan of action:

_____

_____

_____

_____

Wisdom Pearl No. _____

Plan of action:

_____

_____

_____

_____

Resource Materials

CD SERIES

- ❑ Leadership Training Summit 2013
- ❑ Praise Series: The Value Of A Praise; Going Public With My Praise
- ❑ Vision Series: You're About To See What You Saw; Running With Vision; Don't Be Fooled By The Size Of My Cloud
- ❑ Anointing: I'm Too Fat For This Yoke; I'm Anointed To Slay Giants
- ❑ Breaking The Code of Silence: Because I Said So

CD SINGLES

- ❑ I Feel Another Victory On The Way
- ❑ Destroying The Spirit Of Sabotage
- ❑ GOD: The Hard Things Specialist
- ❑ Recover All
- ❑ I'm Not Going Out Like This
- ❑ Don't Let It Kill You Shake It Off
- ❑ Destiny Under Pressure
- ❑ The Great Escape
- ❑ Field Of Favor
- ❑ High Expectations
- ❑ God Wants Me Rich

About Dr. Venice L. McCoy

As a *Destiny Agent*, Dr. McCoy serves the kingdom of God as a change coach and an excellence developer. She is a much sought after speaker, prolific Bible teacher, profound preacher, pioneering and time-less anchor in the Kingdom of God. She is a mentor, a motivator, an innovator, and a true beacon of inspiration.

Being raised in a pastor's home has inimitably equipped Dr. McCoy to share her passion and purpose of helping others to reach their destiny. Her years of service in ministry and the marketplace span the spectrum of more than two decades. She is the founding pastor of the Eagle-Eye International Church and founder of Eagle-Eye Ministries Kingdom Conferences, in Chicago, IL.

Dr. McCoy carries a strong prophetic anointing and powerful message of healing and restoration that touches the lives of families, singles married couples and senior citizens alike. As a twenty-first century leader, Dr. McCoy continuously seeks way in which she can contribute to the Kingdom of God. Her motto is "it can be done".

Dr. McCoy's educational background includes a Ph.D. in Religious Philosophy from Tabernacle Bible College & Seminary and a B.A. in communication from DePaul University.

Stay connected with Dr. McCoy:

www.eagle-eyeministries.com

P.O. Box 734, Blue Island, IL 60406

877.409.1144

wisdompearls21@aol.com

drvml   @drvenicem

When in the Chicago Area
worship with

Eagle-Eye International Church
Venice L. McCoy, Ph.D.-Pastor

1259 S. Kedvale ~ Chicago, IL 60623
Sunday ~ 9:30 a.m. / Wednesday ~ 7:00 p.m.